D0229930

Schools Library Service

550975

100% TWILIGHT BOYS: THE UNOFFICIAL GUIDE

A BANTAM BOOK 978-0-857-51070-9

First published in Great Britain by Bantam,
an imprint of Random House Children's Books
A Random House Group Company

Bantam edition published 2011

1 3 5 7 9 10 8 6 4 2

Text copyright © Bantam Books, 2011

Produced by Shubrook Bros. Creative
www.shubrookbros.com

Front Cover: (BG) © Getty images (MAIN) © David Fisher/Rex Features, © JJ Sassine/Newspix/Rex Features, (L to R) © Getty images, © Sipa Press/Rex Features, © Getty images, © Matt Baron/BEI/Rex Features, © Startraks Photo/Rex Features, Back cover: (BG) © Getty images (L to R) © Getty images, © Getty Images, Jim Smeal/BEI/Rex Features, © Getty images, © Most Wanted/Rex Features, © Getty images, © Startraks Photo/Rex Features, © Startraks Photo/Rex Features, © Getty images.

P2-3 and p62-63: (frames bg) © Getty images, (L to R) © Canadian Press/Rex Features, © Getty images, © Startraks Photo/Rex Features, © Startraks Photo/Rex Features, © WestEnd61/Rex Features, © KPA/Zuma/Rex Features, © Sipa Press/Rex Features, (RP BG) © Getty images, © Startraks Photo/Rex Features, © Getty images, © Getty images, © Matt Baron/BEI/Rex Features, © Brad Hunter/Newspix/Rex Features, © Henry Lamb/BEI/Rex Features, p4-5: © Getty images, p7: (BG) © Getty images, Picture Perfect/Rex Features, p8-9 (BG) © Getty images, (L to R) © BDG/Rex Features, © Startraks Photo/Rex Features (x2), p10-11: (BG) © Getty images, (L to R) © Getty images, © Picture Perfect/Rex Features, © Sipa Press/Rex Features, (RP BG) © Getty images, © Theo Kingma/Rex Features, p12-13: (BG) © Getty images, (L to R) © NBCUPHOTOBANK/Rex Features, © Getty images, © Startraks Photo/Rex Features, p14-15: (BG) Getty images, (L) © Startraks Photo/Rex Features, (TR) © Startraks Photo/Rex Features, (BR) © Action Press/Rex Features, p16-17 (BG) © Mark Bauer / Mood Board/Rex Features, (L) © Startraks Photo/Rex Features, (R) © Jim Smeal/BEI/Rex Features, p18: (BG) © Getty images, (MAIN) © Picture Perfect/Rex Features, p19: (BG) © Getty images, (R) © Most Wanted/Rex Features, p20-21: (BG) Getty images, (L to R) © BDG/Rex Features, © Getty images, © Peter West/Rex Features, p22-23: (BG) © Getty images, (L) © Sipa Press/Rex Features, (R) © Startraks Photo/Rex Features, p24: (BG) © OJO Images/Rex Features, (MAIN) © Getty images, p25: (BG) © istock, p26-27: (BG) © istock, (L to R) © Erik Pendzich/Rex/Rex Features, © Billy Farrell Agency/Rex Features, © Startraks Photo/Rex Features, p28: (BG) © Getty images, (WOLF) © Getty images, p29: (BG) © Getty images, (WOLF) © Getty images, (LAUTNER) © Jim Smeal/BEI/Rex Features, p30-31: (BG) Getty images, (L) © Startraks Photo/Rex Features, (R) © Matt Baron/BEI/Rex Features, p32-33: © Getty images (x3), p34-35: (BG) © Mike Daines/Rex Features, (L to R) © Matt Baron/BEI/Rex Features, © BDG/Rex Features, p36: (BG) © Getty images, (MAIN) © Getty images, p37: © Startraks Photo/Rex Features, p38-39: (BG) © Mark Bauer / Mood Board/Rex Features, © Getty images (x2), p40-41: (BG) © Startraks Photo/Rex Features, © Most Wanted/Rex Features (TO BOTTOM) © Getty images (x2), p43: (BG) © Getty images, (MAIN) © Getty images, p44-45: (BG) © Getty images, (L to R) © Getty images (x2), p46-47: (L to R) © Getty images, © Most Wanted/Rex Features, p48-49: © Startraks Photo/Rex Features, p50: © Getty images (x2), p52: (BG) © Getty images, (T) © Matt Baron/BEI/Rex Features, p53: (BG) Getty images, (MAIN) © Jim Smeal/BEI/Rex Features, p54: © John Sciulli/BEI/Rex Features, p55: (BG) © Getty images, (MAIN) © Getty images, p56: © Getty images, p57: (BG) Getty images, Rex Features, p58: (BG) © Mark Bauer / Mood Board/Rex Feature, © Getty images, (MAIN) © Alex J. Berliner/BEI/Rex Features, © Getty images, © Most Wanted/Rex Features, © Getty images, © Reuse throughout: (HEART ICONS, PARCHMENT, SPARKLES, FUR) © Getty images.

All rights reserved. No part of this publication may be reproduced, stored in a retrieval system, or transmitted in any form or by any means, electronic, mechanical, photocopying, recording or otherwise, without the prior permission of the publishers.

Bantam Books are published by
Random House Children's Books,
61–63 Uxbridge Road, London W5 5SA

www.rbooks.co.uk

www.kidsatrandomhouse.co.uk

Addresses for companies within The Random House Group Limited can be found at:
www.randomhouse.co.uk/offices.htm

THE RANDOM HOUSE GROUP Limited Reg. No. 954009

A CIP catalogue record for this book is available from the British Library

Printed in Italy

EAST SUSSEX
SCHOOLS LIBRARY
SERVICE

550975		
Askews & Holts	Oct-2012	
791 PAR	£6.99	

THE UNOFFICIAL GUIDE TO THE TWILIGHT BOYS

100% UNOFFICIAL

The Twilight Boys

CONTENTS

THE Twilight Saga
PHENOMENON

Whether it's smooth skin, bulging biceps or perfect pecs that make you go weak at the knees, we've got a tantalizing Twilight Boys treat in store for you. So, get ready to meet the guys!

Twilight has changed the lives of millions and ever since our favourite characters were brought to life on screen, we've not stopped dreaming about the gorgeous guys who play the supernatural sizzlers in the movies. How did we cope before our regular fix of Edward and Jacob? We've watched *Twilight*, *New Moon* and *Eclipse* thousands of times, and now we have the *Breaking Dawn* movies to sink our teeth into. Fang-tastic!

The Twilight Saga is the thirteenth highest grossing film series ever!

Following the global success of Stephenie Meyer's books, the pressure was on film makers to choose the right actors to portray the much-loved characters. Luckily, they got it just right and Robert Pattinson, Taylor Lautner and co. set our hearts racing from their very first scenes! This saga really does have something, and some guy, for everyone

Did you know?
The characters Edward and Bella are based on Edward Rochester and Jane from *Jane Eyre*.

Vampire
ROBERT
PATTINSON

BORN: 13 May 1986
PLACE OF BIRTH: London, England
STAR SIGN: Taurus
HEIGHT: 6' 1"
EYE COLOUR: Blue/Grey
HAIR COLOUR: Brown

It's rumoured that Rob fell into acting by chance, and we fell for him as soon as he appeared on our screens. He first caught our eye when he won the role of Cedric Diggory in *Harry Potter and The Goblet of Fire*. Tall and lean with amazing eyes, what's not to love?

Rob has an awesome American accent but he is actually a Brit and misses lots of things about home, particularly football – Rob's an Arsenal supporter.

When he's not making hit movies, he likes to play sport and enjoys everything from football to snowboarding. No wonder he's so fit! And to relax, Rob strums the guitar and writes songs.

On top of all that, Rob was also listed in *Time* magazine's '100 Most Influential People in the World'!

A steamy scene from Breaking Dawn.

HEART STOPPER!
Rumours abound that Robert is dating Kristen Stewart. Will we ever know the truth?

Did you know?
Rob recently adopted a puppy from a shelter and named it Bear!

Did you know?

Rob's a big softie – he once cried at an advert for a cold remedy because he was feeling run down!

"My first kiss was when I was 12."
ROBERT

HOT-O-METER!

FANG-TASTICALLY
CUTE!

THIS VAMP SUCKS!

On our scale from 'sucks' to 'cute', rate how hot you think Robert Pattinson is by marking a line across the Hot-o-meter! We're guessing he's vamp-tastic!

Fang FACT

Robert struggled with the baseball scene in *Twilight* and had to have coaching.

> **"What if I'm not the hero? What if I'm the bad guy?"**
>
> EDWARD

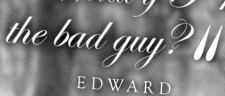

The hair, the eyes, the jawline! This boy has it all!

Did you know?

Robert writes songs under the alias, Bobby Dupea. Two of his compositions can be found on the *Twilight* soundtrack.

Kristen's character, Bella, tests Edward's vampire self-control to the max.

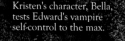

EDWARD CULLEN

PAST NAME: Edward Masen
BORN: 1901
FATHER: Carlisle Cullen (adoptive)
TALENTS: Telepathy
ROMANCE: Bella Swan

Edward Cullen is an enigma from the beginning. A man (or vampire!) of few words, with a chiseled jaw and an extremely intense stare, he's a dark and mysterious stranger who turns heads wherever he goes. He's so good-looking that you'd never guess he's actually over one hundred years old!

Bella was drawn to him straight away and it's easy to see why. But as well as his smooth, pale skin and sparkling, golden eyes, Edward has some special hidden talents, too. Later on he reveals his super-speed and telepathy skills, both of which we're sure could come in handy and they only add to his already-huge appeal. Loyal, protective and totally devoted to the one he loves, Edward would be the picture-perfect boyfriend we all dream of finding. Well, if you can get past his thirst for blood that is!

Edward would never let you down and would do absolutely anything for his true love. Bella, we think you're one very lucky lady!

Did you know?

You can see more of Rob in *Water for Elephants*, and possibly also in *Bel Ami* and *Cosmopolis*.

Werewolf TAYLOR LAUTNER

BORN: 11 February 1992
PLACE OF BIRTH: Grand Rapids, Michigan
STAR SIGN: Aquarius
HEIGHT: 5' 10"
EYE COLOUR: Hazel
HAIR COLOUR: Brown

Taylor took up karate at age 6 and had a black belt by the time he was 8. With those roundhouse kicks, he was perfectly prepared to play a powerful werewolf.

His first audition was for a fast food advert. Although he didn't land the part, he had been bitten by the acting bug.

With tanned skin and those chocolate brown eyes, Taylor must hear wolf-whistles wherever he goes!

Taylor gets the trophy but his character can't get the girl!

HEART STOPPER!
Taylor is so cute he even makes his own Valentine's Day cards. Ah, bless him!

Taylor is always happy for a quick photo with the fans.

"I want to find a girl that is herself. I don't want someone that pretends."

TAYLOR

HOT-O-METER!

WOLF-TASTICALLY
GORGEOUS!

On our scale from 'fur-get it' to 'gorgeous', rate how hot you think Taylor Lautner is by marking a line across the Hot-o-meter! He can only be gorgeous, right?

FUR-GET IT!

Furry FACT

To prepare for the role, Taylor hung out with kids from the real Quileute tribe.

Did you know?

Taylor hated wearing a wig to play Jacob as it was itchy and hot and got caught in his food!

> "Have you ever had a secret you couldn't tell anyone?"
>
> JACOB

Did you know?

We're so excited to see Taylor in the film *Stretch Armstrong*. He certainly does have strong arms!

Did you know?

His first paid job was a commercial for Nickelodeon advertising *The Rugrats Movie*.

Did you know?

Taylor's most prized possession is his martial arts Warrior Cup trophy.

Taylor and Jacob share a passion for motorbikes.

CHARACTER PROFILE

JACOB BLACK

FATHER: Billy Black
MOTHER: Sarah Black
TALENTS: Telepathy with the pack
ROMANCE: Bella Swan

Jacob Black lights up the screen with his super-cute smile and totally sets it on fire whenever he takes off his shirt.

Even his best friend Bella has to admit that he's got a smoking-hot body and she says out loud what we were all secretly thinking, 'Hello, biceps!'

With his chilled out, positive attitude, Jacob would make any girl feel happy and really relaxed. He has also got a few exhilarating hobbies, such as repairing and racing motorbikes and diving off cliffs, so with him you can be sure that the excitement would never end!

Best friends, Bella and Jacob.

He has an amazing six-pack and we can certainly see why Bella was tempted to become more than just good friends; he really is a hottie...

ARE YOU...
Team
EDWARD

Check out whether you're more Team Edward or Team Jacob by answering the questions below. Good luck!

1
On a romantic date you prefer to:
A. Eat loads of good food ☐
B. Dance under the stars ☐

2
You like guys who drive . . .
A. Fast motorbikes ☐
B. Fast cars ☐

3
On a sunny day, you prefer your guy to:
A. Hit the sun lounger ☐
B. Chill indoors ☐

4
Your dream guys is:
A. Your best friend ☐
B. Your soul mate ☐

5
You like boys with . . .
A. Similar interests to you ☐
B. A world of knowledge ☐

6
With your guy you like to:
A. Dive off a cliff ☐
B. Relax in a meadow ☐

OR...
Team
JACOB

7 You love a boy who has . . .

A. Golden skin ☐

B. Golden eyes ☐

8 Your ideal boy is . . .

A. Close to his friends ☐

B. Close to his family ☐

9 You like your boy to have:

A. A super-buff body ☐

B. A totally-toned torso ☐

10 Your guy likes you because you are:

A. An open book ☐

B. A bit of a mystery ☐

answers

MOSTLY As

You're TEAM JACOB!

You love a guy with a ripped body and a great sense of adventure.

MOSTLY Bs

You're TEAM EDWARD!

You love a guy who is quiet, elusive and prefers to stay in the shadows.

MEET...

THE
Cullen BOYS

When the Cullens moved to Forks, they brought a whole world of weirdness with them. You might think this mysterious family are pretty messed up, but we love the Olympic coven of 'veggie' vampires!

Keeping to themselves and rarely venturing into the sunlight, the Cullen clan seems to have some scary secrets . . . But when the truth is revealed, we see that these vampires are caring, gentle creatures. In fact, the Cullens are one cool family!

ROBERT V EDWARD

At first glance, actor Robert Pattinson and character Edward Cullen don't appear to have much in common. One is in his mid-twenties, loves acting and struggles to strike a baseball, and the other is over one hundred years old, has skin as cold as stone and can hit a home run every time.

But they do share some things. Both Robert and Edward love music and can play the piano. Edward loves Bella Swan and Rob is reportedly romancing Kristen Stewart, who plays her role. And of course, Robert and Edward are equally gorgeous!

Did you know?
Robert and Edward are both fantastic pianists.

" I always like a kind of madness in a woman..."
ROBERT

" It's wrong. It's not safe. I'm dangerous, Bella — please, grasp that. "
EDWARD

Vampire
KELLAN
L U T Z

BORN: 15 March 1985
PLACE OF BIRTH: Dickinson, North Dakota
STAR SIGN: Pisces
HEIGHT: 6' 1"
EYE COLOUR: Blue
HAIR COLOUR: Light brown

It's hard to believe, but Kellan is even hotter in real life than he is as vampire Emmett. He has huge muscles from working out and playing sports and prefers to perform his own movie stunts if possible. We love watching beefy Kellan in action!

He decided uni wasn't for him and that his dream was to act. He got his big break as a regular on US TV soap *The Bold and the Beautiful* and the show's title is pretty appropriate; Kellan seems both bold *and* beautiful to us . . .

Kellan takes a stroll in the sun after another great workout.

Did you know?

In 2004, super-hot Kellan fronted the Summer Catalogue of Abercrombie and Fitch.

HOT-O-METER!

FANG-TASTICALLY
CUTE!

THIS VAMP
SUCKS!

On our scale from 'sucks' to 'cute', rate how hot you think Kellan Lutz is by marking a line across the Hot-o-meter! We're guessing this vamp actor will send your pulse racing!

A lot of girls think they have flaws that really aren't flaws.

KELLAN

HEART STOPPER!
Sadly, Kellan is rumoured to be dating gorgeous 90210 actress AnnaLynne McCord.

CHARACTER PROFILE

EMMETT CULLEN

PAST NAME: Emmett McCarty
BORN: 1915
FATHER: Carlisle Cullen (adoptive)
TALENTS: Physical strength
ROMANCE: Rosalie Hale (wife)

If you're into fun and fit guys, then Emmett's the one for you. With a great sense of humour, he's the joker of the Cullen family.

He's strong, protective and willing to throw himself in front of werewolves or other vampires to save someone he loves. Just don't challenge him to an arm wrestle; you wouldn't stand a chance against his bulging biceps! But under that tough exterior, Emmett's a big softie and he can wrap those enormous arms around us anytime.

Vampire JACKSON RATHBONE

BORN: 21 December 1984
PLACE OF BIRTH: Singapore
STAR SIGN: Sagittarius
HEIGHT: 5' 10"
EYE COLOUR: Brown
HAIR COLOUR: Brown

Jackson studied acting at school before moving to LA. His creativity doesn't stop at acting though; he's really musical, too. Jackson plays guitar, harmonica and keyboards, and he's also in a band called *100 Monkeys*. Who doesn't love a boy in a rock band?

Cool, quirky Jackson names heartthrob Johnny Depp as his hero and inspiration, which we can see from his wild hairstyle and alternative fashion sense.

HEART STOPPER!
Jackson likes women with a sincere smile, a love for the arts and sense of adventure.

Fang **FACT**
Jackson researched the American Civil War to really understand his character's background.

Stylish and funny . . . We love you Jacks!

HOT-O-METER!

FANG-TASTICALLY
CUTE!

On our scale from 'sucks' to 'cute', rate how hot you think Jackson Rathbone is by marking a line across the Hot-o-meter! Come on, check out that cute pout!

THIS VAMP SUCKS!

"He's a vampire barely able to control himself but he does it for love."

JACKSON

CHARACTER PROFILE

JASPER HALE

PAST NAME: Jasper Whitlock
BORN: 1843
FATHER: Carlisle Cullen (adoptive)

TALENTS: Emotion manipulation
ROMANCE: Alice Cullen (wife)

Quite quiet and really reserved with brooding good looks, Jasper is the most serious member of the Cullen family. He's a deep thinker and a great listener, two qualities that we think would make him a brilliant boyfriend. Smouldering Jasper would stare deeply into your eyes and make you feel like the only girl in the world.

If you were ever feeling stressed out or a little anxious, Jasper would soon lighten the mood and help you to relax, by using his calming, emotion manipulation talent. To us, that sounds like pure bliss!

23

Vampire
PETER
FACINELLI

BORN: 26 November 1973
PLACE OF BIRTH: Ozone Park, New York
STAR SIGN: Sagittarius
HEIGHT: 5' 10"
EYE COLOUR: Hazel
HAIR COLOUR: Brown

At 16, Peter went to the Atlantic Theater Company Acting School in New York. His first role was on *Law and Order* and he went on to appear in movies such as *The Scorpion King*.

He's now been immortalized as Dr. Carlisle, the head of the Cullen clan. Like his *Twilight* character, Peter's a real family man and loves to play football with his three daughters.

He's slightly older than the other Cullen boys, but we still love this hot doc!

Did you know?
Peter is married to beautiful 90210 star Jennie Garth.

HOT-O-METER!

FANG-TASTICALLY CUTE!

THIS VAMP SUCKS!

On our scale from 'sucks' to 'cute', rate how hot you think Peter Facinelli is by marking a line across the Hot-o-meter! He's the vamp doctor we surely all love.

CHARACTER PROFILE

DR. CARLISLE CULLEN

PAST NAME: Carlisle Cullen (Anglican pastor)
BORN: 1643
FATHER: Name unknown
TALENTS: Compassion
ROMANCE: Esme Cullen (wife)

Carlisle is calm, kind-natured and softly spoken. He rescued each member of the Cullen family when they were gravely ill or in serious trouble, going on to marry Esme and adopt the others.

Carlisle works at Forks hospital and is a truly talented doctor. With his youthful appearance, it's hard to believe that he has centuries of medical experience! Why can't all doctors look like him?

VAMPIRE HUNT

You may be a fan of the boys who play your favourite *Twilight* characters, but how many of their character's names can you find in this word search?

Carlisle   *Laurent*   *Edward*   *Demetri*

Emmett   *Riley*   *Jasper*   *Caius*

```
A C E M M E T T X K R
K E D L A N H A S J A
X C W B X E E R Y A X
F C A R L I S L E S L
A N R A R R Y A O P R
C C D X A V I U R E T
V A C K S O K R S R S
R I L E Y U A E Y I Y
R U Y T A Y L N R M
T S A D E M E T R I
```

THE Love Triangle

Whether you're Team Edward or Team Jacob, you've got to agree that they're both super-hot. Bella had to choose between them, so let's check out what they each bring to the romantic table.

Edward

Edward and Bella's love is what every girl dreams about. Edward is the picture-perfect guy that you very rarely find. He's really romantic and very old-school when it comes to dating.

Your parents probably wouldn't approve of you dating Edward though, because he's quiet, intense and mysterious. To them, he might even seem a little dangerous . . .

But Bella is attracted to his loyalty and his unconditional love for her. She believes Edward is her soul mate and that she needs him to survive, even if it means sacrificing her human life.

Jacob

Jacob is very grounded, kind and good-natured. He's fun and friendly and always knows how to make a girl feel relaxed and at ease. On a date with Jacob, there's sure to be lots of laughs.

Open and honest, with that cheeky 'boy next door' appeal, he is definitely the one that your parents would want you to go out with.

Jacob quickly becomes Bella's best mate, although he desires something more. He provides her with the friendship and warmth that she craves but is always left wondering what could have been . . .

MEET...

THE
wolf pack
BOYS

If you can get over the sudden shape-shifting, then these buff boys have a lot to offer. With their matching tattoos and cliff diving, some would say they are a totally-cool crew. We'd agree with that!

This gang of gorgeous guys live in La Push. As a pack of werewolves, it's their sworn duty to protect the people of Forks against vampires. They generally keep to themselves but if they were ever seen in town, they'd certainly attract plenty of wolf-whistles!

Did you know?

The guys who play characters in the wolf pack are also friends off set, too.

Taylor Lautner once said that he felt he's a lot like his *Twilight* character. They both have a strong sense of adventure, a love of the outdoors and enjoy riding fast motorbikes. No wonder Taylor enjoyed playing the role of Jacob!

And the likenesses don't end there. Both are loyal, friendly guys, with big hearts and smiles. We're happy to hear that Taylor and our favourite werewolf have so many sizzling similarities!

"The most important quality a girl can have is honesty."

TAYLOR

"Well, I'm sorry I can't be the right kind of monster for you, Bella."

JACOB

Furry FACT

When the boys phase, they can become moodier due to their ferocious wolf side.

Werewolf
KIOWA
GORDON

BORN: 25 March 1990
PLACE OF BIRTH: Berlin, Germany
STAR SIGN: Aries
HEIGHT: 5' 11"
EYE COLOUR: Brown
HAIR COLOUR: Black

With his boyish charm and good looks, it's no wonder Kiowa ended up in front of the movie cameras.

In the original *Twilight* movie, the part of Embry was played by Krys Hyatt, but Kiowa impressed the casting director so much that he landed the role for the other films.

Fame hasn't gone to his head and he's still a very grounded guy. We're glad sweet, shy Kiowa will be on our screens for the rest of the series!

Did you know?

Stephenie Meyer and Kiowa go to the same church and she recommended he audition for Embry.

HOT-O-METER!

WOLF-TASTICALLY GORGEOUS!

FUR-GET IT!

On our scale from 'fur-get it' to 'gorgeous', rate how hot you think Kiowa Gordon is by marking a line across the Hot-o-meter! Check out those boyish good looks!

" *We spend an hour in makeup... they enhanced our abs.* "

KIOWA

Furry FACT
Before *Twilight*, Kiowa naturally had long hair. He had to have it cut for the movie.

CHARACTER PROFILE

EMBRY CALL

FATHER: Unknown
MOTHER: Mrs Call

TALENTS: Speed
IMPRINTS ON: Unknown

Cute and caring, Embry is the boy next door that you'd definitely want to be friends with. Although he's a reserved, quiet and shy member of the werewolf gang, he's also playful, full of fun and Jacob Black's very best bud.

Embry is gentle, loyal, thoughtful and a great listener. With those four top traits, as well as his slender body and dark, smouldering looks, we think any girl would be lucky to have this gorgeous guy in her life!

HEART STOPPER!
Kiowa has a soft spot for the romantic movie *Valentine's Day* which stars his off set buddy, Taylor Lautner.

Werewolf
TYSON
HOUSEMAN

BORN: 9 February 1990
PLACE OF BIRTH: Edmonton, Canada
STAR SIGN: Aquarius
HEIGHT: 5' 9"
EYE COLOUR: Brown
HAIR COLOUR: Black

Tyson is new to the film world and his only roles before the *Twilight* movies were in plays at high school, where he also trained in combat sports like fighting and fencing. He loves working out and hits the gym around five times a week. No wonder Tyson's torso is so toned!

He's a massive fan of extreme sports but his ultimate hero isn't a huge sports star as you would imagine – it's actually his mum! Tyson is toned, sporty *and* sweet . . . Swoon!

Did you know?

Tyson saw the advert for the open audition on the internet and he didn't even know what the movie was going to be.

HOT-O-METER!

WOLF-TASTICALLY GORGEOUS!

On our scale from 'fur-get it' to 'gorgeous', rate how hot you think Tyson Houseman is by marking a line across the Hot-o-meter! Quil he be your number one?

FUR-GET IT!

!!*I only had a minute part in New Moon, but in Eclipse my part was way bigger.*!!

TYSON

CHARACTER PROFILE

QUIL ATEARA

FATHER: Quil Ateara Jr.
MOTHER: Unknown
TALENTS: Usual pack traits
IMPRINTS ON: Claire

Jacob's other best friend, Quil, is the sizzling shape-shifter with a huge heart. He doesn't make much of an appearance in the first three films but with his cute, cheeky grin, we think we are due to see more of Quil in the *Breaking Dawn* movies.

Quil is bursting with excitement and enthusiasm which is totally infectious. When in his werewolf form, his chocolate brown fur is said to be a reflection of his sweet personality, and what girl doesn't like a sweet treat every now and then?

Furry FACT

Tyson is so close with his fellow wolf actors he calls them his 'pack brothers'.

Werewolf
BOOBOO
STEWART

BORN: 21 January 1994
PLACE OF BIRTH: Beverly Hills, USA
STAR SIGN: Aquarius
HEIGHT: 5' 8"
EYE COLOUR: Brown
HAIR COLOUR: Black

Booboo has appeared in several indie movies both as an actor and a stunt man. The super-strong star is also a Junior Martial Arts World Champion and a massive wrestling fan; he loves having his photo taken with his WWE idols.

Music is another of his passions and he used to be in a band called *Echoes of Angels*.

He first played werewolf Seth in *Eclipse* and we can't wait to watch beautiful Booboo in action again in *Breaking Dawn!*

HEART STOPPER!
Booboo once said his celebrity crush was Adriana Lima.

HOT-O-METER!

WOLF-TASTICALLY GORGEOUS!

On our scale from 'fur-get it' to 'gorgeous', rate how hot you think Booboo Stewart is by marking a line across the Hot-o-meter! That face must melt your heart!

FUR-GET IT!

Did you know?

Booboo appears in the Martial Arts Junior Hall of Fame after winning back-to-back titles.

Furry **FACT**

Stephenie Meyer used the name Seth for this character because it was her brother's name.

Booboo looks hot in fiery red!

CHARACTER PROFILE

SETH CLEARWATER

FATHER: Harry Clearwater
MOTHER: Sue Clearwater

TALENTS: Ultra-hearing
IMPRINTS ON: Unknown

Seth may be the youngest member of the werewolf pack, but he's still packing some pecs! He's a super-slender shape-shifter and always has a huge, happy grin on his face. With his youthful, energetic and cheerful personality, self-assured Seth is sure to make any girl feel on top of the world and as though absolutely anything is possible.

Seth is extremely loyal and he never gives up on what he believes in. He totally idolises Jacob but he also becomes really good pals with vampire Edward, and of course any friend of theirs is most definitely a friend of ours, too!

Werewolves

CHASKE SPENCER

BORN: 9 March 1975
PLACE OF BIRTH: Tahlequah, Oklahoma
STAR SIGN: Pisces
HEIGHT: 6' 3"
EYE COLOUR: Brown
HAIR COLOUR: Black

Chaske dreamed of being a photographer but decided to pursue a career in front of the camera. We're glad he did, or we'd never have seen this gorgeous guy's true talent!

Between auditions he worked as a waiter before swapping serving rolls for acting roles!

Having played a vampire on stage and now a werewolf on screen, Chaske clearly has a thing for supernatural characters, and so do we!

HOT-O-METER!

WOLF-TASTICALLY GORGEOUS!   FUR-GET IT!

CHARACTER PROFILE

SAM ULEY

FATHER: Joshua Uley
MOTHER: Mrs. Uley
TALENTS: Leading
IMPRINTS ON: Emily Young

Sam is a strong and supportive shape-shifter who's tall and broad with delicious, dark eyes. He is the most mature member of the werewolf pack and, as the acknowledged leader, the others really respect him.

Sam is proud and protective of his pack and any girl would feel so safe and secure when wrapped up in his amazingly muscular arms, complete with the tribe tattoo. This awesome Alpha can give us a huge hug any time he likes!

Did you know?

Chaske's name is of Native American origin and means 'first born son'.

BRONSON
PELLETIER

BORN: 31 December 1986
PLACE OF BIRTH: Vancouver Island, Canada
STAR SIGN: Capricorn
HEIGHT: 5' 11"
EYE COLOUR: Brown
HAIR COLOUR: Brown

After watching the movie *Underworld*, Bronson dreamed of playing a werewolf, and luckily he landed the role of Jared in the *Twilight* films. He has four brothers, so is used to being part of a pack!

With his wide range of hobbies, including camping, snowboarding and listening to punk rock, life with buff Bronson would never be boring.

Previously an actor in Canadian TV show *Renegadepress.com*, Bronson says he's honoured to now be part of such a popular big screen project.

HOT-O-METER!

WOLF-TASTICALLY
GORGEOUS!

FUR-GET
IT!

CHARACTER PROFILE
JARED CAMERON

FATHER: Unknown
MOTHER: Unknown
TALENTS: Superior sight
IMPRINTS ON: Kim

Although Jared is quite a young member of the pack, he is self-assured and full of confidence. He's a bit of a joker who likes to mess around and he is loved by the boys in the tribe for his light-hearted nature and his consideration for others.

Jared also likes to make a bet or two and we'll wager that this werewolf is one to watch out for in *Breaking Dawn*. His talent is supersight, and what girl wouldn't fall in love with this cool character at first sight?

Werewolf
ALEX
MERAZ

BORN: 10 January 1985
PLACE OF BIRTH: Mesa, Arizona
STAR SIGN: Capricorn
HEIGHT: 5' 11"
EYE COLOUR: Brown
HAIR COLOUR: Black

Alex is an all-round creative guy and loves painting and illustrating as well as acting. He once created his own comic book and also worked as an art teacher. With other passions that include; martial arts, wrestling, and break dancing, it's no wonder he has such a buff body!

Alex actually auditioned for the role of Sam in the *Twilight* films, but was so intense on screen that the casting directors thought he'd be better as the bad-boy of the pack. With his gorgeous glare, we think they were right!

"I enjoy every aspect of it. I'm just fortunate to be a part of it."
ALEX

HEART STOPPER!
We're sure Alex is a huge romantic, but he's not a big fan of all romantic movies. On a date you'd have to choose your film wisely!

Furry FACT
Alex and Taylor often go to the gym together and share workout tips.

CHARACTER PROFILE

PAUL LAHOTE

FATHER: Unknown
MOTHER: Unknown
TALENTS: Enhanced senses
IMPRINTS ON: Rachel Black

Tall, dark and handsome, Paul is dominating and a little bit dangerous. Not only is he cool, confident and cocky, he is also the most volatile werewolf in the pack with an angry attitude and a very short fuse!

Although he sometimes struggles to keep control, Paul is a completely loyal and faithful to his friends and is willing to do anything to protect the pack. Even with his fiery temper, what girl could resist the charms of this hot hunk?

Did you know?

Alex once formed a dance group who specialised in performing indigenous dance.

HOT-O-METER!

WOLF-TASTICALLY GORGEOUS!

FUR-GET IT!

On our scale from 'fur-get it' to 'gorgeous', rate how hot you think Alex Meraz is by marking a line across the Hot-o-meter! He's certainly a passionate guy.

SUPERNATURAL
SUITOR

Start here →

Where do you belong in the world of Twilight? Answer the questions below to find out whether you're better suited to the Cullens, the pack or the high school guys.

A boy with unusual coloured eyes asks you out. Do you:
A. SAY YES?
B. TELL HIM YOU'RE WASHING YOUR HAIR?

A →

On a dinner date, would your boyfriend:
A. NOT EAT A THING?
B. CLEAR HIS PLATE?

A →

It's a bright, sunny day. Do you:
A. STAY INSIDE?
B. GET OUT AND ABOUT?

What movies do you like best?
A. ACTION OR HORROR.
B. ROMANCE OR COMEDY.

A →

Do you:
A. LIKE SOME ALONE TIME?
B. PREFER TO BE A SOCIAL BUTTERFLY?

A →

Do you like to:
A. TRAVEL THE WORLD?
B. STAY LOCAL?

Are you:
A. QUIET AND SERIOUS?
B. LOUD AND ADVENTUROUS?

B →

Does your boyfriend:
A. DRIVE A CAR?
B. RIDE A MOTORBIKE?

B →

Are you looking for:
A. TRUE LOVE?
B. LASTING FRIENDSHIP?

You love boys who are:
A. PALE AND TONED.
B. TANNED AND MUSCULAR.

A

A

B

A

You prefer your boyfriend to be:
A. COOL.
B. HOT.

A

A

B

A

Does your boyfriend have any secrets?
A. YES, HE'S A COMPLETE MYSTERY.
B. NO, HE'S TOTALLY UPFRONT AND HONEST.

B

B

Your boyfriend doesn't have fangs or fur. Do you:
A. SWAP HIM FOR A SUPERNATURAL SIZZLER?
B. STICK WITH YOUR HUMAN HOTTIE?

B

You are...
CHILLING WITH THE CULLEN'S
You're definitely Edward's girl. You love his mystique, charm and knowledge of the world. He's totally intense, but you just can't get enough of him!

You are...
RUNNING WITH THE WOLF PACK
Jacob is the guy for you. You love his warmth and spirit of adventure. Even when he's a werewolf, you're happy to snuggle into that fur. Now, that's true love!

You are...
HANGING WITH THE HIGH SCHOOL GUYS
So, you actually prefer a human hottie to a supernatural sizzler after all! Whether Mike, Eric or Tyler is more your type, you love him for his safe, sensitive and sensible nature.

MEET...

THE
bad boy
VAMP

It's time to check out three of the most terrifying vampires in town! If you're drawn to bad boys then look no further, as they don't come much meaner than this bunch of blood-suckers.

Laurent, James and Riley are the scariest vampires outside of the Volturi, and they're also some of the hottest. With their piercing eyes and chiseled faces, it's easy to forget that these gorgeous guys are only after one thing – human blood, and lots of it!

Vampire
EDI GATHEGI

BORN: 10 March 1979
PLACE OF BIRTH: Nairobi, Kenya
STAR SIGN: Pisces
HEIGHT: 6' 1"
EYE COLOUR: Brown
HAIR COLOUR: Brown

Edi's lifelong dream was to become a pro basketball player until he injured his knee. He then set his heart on acting and has appeared in many movies and TV shows.

When he auditioned for the *Twilight* films, Edi had never heard of the series and didn't know his character was a vampire.

Edi's talents don't stop at acting though – rumour has it he can do an awesome Michael Jackson impression. We think that edible Edi doing the m o o n w a l k would be well worth seeing!

HOT-O-METER!

FANG-TASTICALLY **CUTE!**

THIS VAMP SUCKS!

CHARACTER PROFILE
LAURENT

PAST NAME: Laurent
BORN: Around 1700
FATHER: Unknown

TALENTS: Vampire powers
ROMANCE: Irina

With his calm, quiet demeanor, enormous eyes and long, dark dreadlocks, Laurent really is one cool character. He seems to be a self-serving and power-hungry vampire, who displays very little loyalty and is always looking out for number one.

But sometimes, just sometimes, he appears to have a good heart after all . . . Those girls who go for gorgeous guys with lots of confidence, charm and charisma will just love luscious Laurent!

Vampire
CAM
GIGANDET

BORN: 16 August 1982
PLACE OF BIRTH: Tacoma, Washington
STAR SIGN: Leo
HEIGHT: 6'
EYE COLOUR: Blue
HAIR COLOUR: Brown

Early in his career, cute Cam was quickly cast as the bad boy and fulfilled this role in the TV series *The O.C.* and *CSI: Crime Scene Investigation* before being destined to play James in *Twilight*.

Cam's a sporty guy who loves spending his 'down time' skiing, surfing and practicing self-defense, all of which make Cam super-strong as well as super-hot.

He also enjoys being outside and likes strolling around LA at dusk. If you ever fancy some company on those long walks, Cam, just give us a call!

Did you know?

Cam won a 'One to Watch' award at the 10th Annual Young Hollywood Awards.

HOT-O-METER!

FANG-TASTICALLY CUTE!

THIS VAMP SUCKS!

On our scale from 'sucks' to 'cute', rate how hot you think Cam Gigandet is by marking a line across the Hot-o-meter! Surely, Cam's got to be one of the hottest boys around!

> **"There's an air of mystery that surrounds vampires… guys long to be viewed that way."**
> CAM

HEART STOPPER!
He enjoys long walks on the beach at sunset. What a romantic!

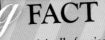

Fang FACT
Cam originally fancied the part of Emmett but decided he had to be James after reading the book.

CHARACTER PROFILE

JAMES

PAST NAME: James
BORN: 1780
FATHER: Unknown (French trapper)
TALENTS: Tracking sense
ROMANCE: Victoria

Muscular and merciless, James is the long-haired lovely who's definitely not to be messed with. He may look cute but James can be cunning and also extremely cruel at times.

James is a truly talented tracker who rarely fails to find what, or who, he's searching for. Girls, this is one gorgeous guy who would never, ever give up on you, no matter what!

Vampire
XAVIER
S A M U E L

BORN: 10 December 1983
PLACE OF BIRTH: Victoria, Australia
STAR SIGN: Sagittarius
HEIGHT: 5' 9"
EYE COLOUR: Brown
HAIR COLOUR: Brown

avier grew up in Australia where he attended drama school. When he wasn't busy studying, this multi-talented guy spent his time singing in a band before heading to Hollywood.

His first movie role was in *2:37*, an indie film that was highly acclaimed. Since then he has appeared in a few feature films, including *September* and *Newcastle*, but it was when he landed the role of Riley in the *Twilight* movies that he really got his big break, and one very bad vampire was born.

Did you know?

He plays the keyboard and used to be in a band called *Hyatus* back at uni.

"I kinda wish that Riley was a member of the Cullen family 'cause they're all so lovely."
XAVIER

FANG-TASTICALLY CUTE!

THIS VAMP SUCKS!

On our scale from 'sucks' to 'cute', rate how hot you think Xavier Samuel is by marking a line across the Hot-o-meter! We think he's one hot, Aussie hunk!

Fang FACT

Xavier was initiated into the cast by playing a *Twilight* board game to test his knowledge.

HEART STOPPER!

Xavier is dating Shermine Shahrivar who won Miss Europe 2005.

CHARACTER PROFILE

R I L E Y

PAST NAME: Riley Biers
BORN: 1990
CREATED BY: Victoria

TALENTS: Self-control
ROMANCE: Victoria

 s a human, Riley is hot. As a vampire, Riley is hot and dangerous!

Tall and tough, with shiny dark blond hair and very handsome features, vampire Riley is devastatingly attractive. Although he can be pretty unpredictable and sometimes a little aggressive, he also comes across as affectionate, attentive and quite caring at times.

Faithful and fearless, Riley is someone you can always rely on. This is one buff bad boy who will remain loyal right to the end and would do absolutely anything for the girl he loves . . .

SPOT THE DIFFERENCE

Can you spot the 10 differences in the bottom picture of Taylor looking incredibly cool?

Twilight Saga
CROSSWORD

It's time to test your knowledge of Twilight trivia!

ACROSS

3. Character played by Kiowa Gordon
4. Surname of the Olympic coven
7. The pack Jacob belongs to
9. Vampire who almost kills Bella in Twilight
10. Leah's younger brother
11. Strongest of the Cullens

DOWN

1. The girl caught in the love triangle
2. Billy's son
5. Name of the third book and movie
6. 3000 year old vampire coven
8. The vampire who falls for Bella
9. Last survivor of the Southern vampire wars

MEET...

Volturi
THE

The unofficial 'royal family' of vampires has been around for over 3000 years. Beware as you enter their dark den, as they are the the most sinister supernatural beings you'll ever encounter.

Enforcing the vampire laws from the Italian city of Volterra, the Volturi are the oldest coven in the world. They have a scary reputation and rule by fear. With their super talents, these powerful creatures are certainly not to be messed with . . .

Vampire
JAMES
CAMPBELL BOWER

BORN: 22 November 1988
PLACE OF BIRTH: London, England
STAR SIGN: Sagittarius
HEIGHT: 6'
EYE COLOUR: Blue
HAIR COLOUR: Blond

 hilst still at school, James played the part of Anthony in *Sweeney Todd: The Demon Barber of Fleet Street*. He then appeared in Guy Richie's *RocknRolla*, before becoming Caius in the *Twilight* movies.

This London lad is triple-talented – he's a singer and model as well as an actor. He is the super-hot lead singer of a band called *The Darling Buds* and loves to listen to *Biffy Clyro*. We can't wait to see him, whether it's on the catwalk, stage or screen!

Did you know?

James plays Gellert Grindelwald in *Harry Potter and the Deathly Hallows*.

HOT-O-METER!

FANG-TASTICALLY CUTE!

THIS VAMP SUCKS!

CHARACTER PROFILE

C A I U S

PAST NAME: Unknown
BORN: Around 1300 BC
TALENTS: Usual vampire traits
OCCUPATION: Volturi leader
ROMANCE: Athenodora

Caius is the youngest and by far the hottest of the three Volturi leaders, but he is also extremely cruel and merciless and has a selfish, stubborn streak.

With his perfect, pale skin, dangerously dark eyes and light, shoulder-length hair, Caius is pretty cute, even for an evil vampire. This cool character values the lives of those he loves most, and he is definitely the Volturi leader that we love most.

Vampires
MICHAEL
SHEEN

BORN: 5 February 1969
PLACE OF BIRTH: Newport, Wales
STAR SIGN: Aquaruis
HEIGHT: 5' 10"
EYE COLOUR: Green
HAIR COLOUR: Brown

Michael is a well-established Welsh actor who has portrayed many famous figures in his time, including: Tony Blair, David Frost and Brian Clough. He is also no stranger to vampire and werewolf films as he played Lucian in the *Underworld* movies.

HOT-O-METER!
FANG-TASTICALLY CUTE!
THIS VAMP SUCKS!

CHARACTER PROFILE
ARO

BORN: Around 1300 BC
BIRTH PLACE: Greece
TALENTS: Tactile telepathy
OCCUPATION: Volturi leader
ROMANCE: Sulpicia

Spine-chilling Aro is the accepted leader of the Volturi. He has the ability to read any thought a person has ever had by simply touching them. On the outside he is polite and gentlemanly but inside he is filled with the most deadly of thoughts!

CHRISTOPHER
HEYERDAHL

BORN: 17 October 1961
PLACE OF BIRTH: British Columbia, Canada
STAR SIGN: Libra
HEIGHT: 6' 4"
EYE COLOUR: Blue
HAIR COLOUR: Brown

Christopher has been an actor of stage and screen for over 25 years and has worked across the world, including Asia, Africa, Europe and North America. He has made regular appearances on the *Stargate Atlantis* TV series amongst others and we hope to see more of him in the *Breaking Dawn* movies.

HOT-O-METER!
FANG-TASTICALLY CUTE!
THIS VAMP SUCKS!

CHARACTER PROFILE
MARCUS

BORN: Around 1350 BC
BIRTH PLACE: Greece
TALENTS: Relational empathy
OCCUPATION: Voluti leader
ROMANCE: Didyme

Marcus is one of the three leaders of the Volturi. He doesn't say much, but what he does say is often out of necessity rather than passion. Style wise, Marcus has long, flowing hair that seems to be the Volturi leader in-house style.

CAMERON
B R I G H T

BORN: 26 January 1993
PLACE OF BIRTH: Victoria, Canada
STAR SIGN: Aquarius
HEIGHT: 5' 10" (178cm)
EYE COLOUR: Blue
HAIR COLOUR: Brown

Did you know?
Cameron wants to learn how to be a motor mechanic.

Cute Cameron was born in Canada and as far as we know, he always wanted to be an actor. He started off by appearing in television adverts, before he moved on to TV shows and finally into films. His first major movie role was in the horror film *Godsend*, starring Robert De Niro. Not bad company to be keeping at the age of 10!

He was then cast as evil Alec in the *Twilight* movies, with Dakota Fanning playing his twin sister, Jane. Cameron can't wait for the action scenes in *Breaking Dawn*, and neither can we!

CHARACTER PROFILE
A L E C

PAST NAME: Unknown
BORN: Pre-800 AD
FAMILY: Jane (sister)
TALENTS: Sensory deprivation
OCCUPATION: Volturi guard

Lively and little, Alec may have the face of an angel but he doesn't always behave like one. In fact, underneath the cute exterior is one cool, calculating and extremely evil vampire kid. Together with his sinister twin sister, Jane, Alec has very special powers that allow him to take down and destroy his enemies with ease.

We know he's deceitful and deadly but with his dark good-looks and super-sweet smile, we also think he is downright delicious.

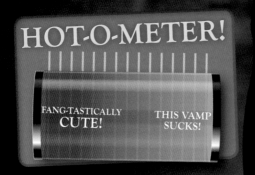

HOT-O-METER!

FANG-TASTICALLY **CUTE!**

THIS VAMP SUCKS!

53

Vampires
CHARLIE BEWLEY

BORN: 25 January 1981
PLACE OF BIRTH: London, England
STAR SIGN: Aquaruis
HEIGHT: 5' 11"
EYE COLOUR: Blue
HAIR COLOUR: Blond

Charlie loves to travel and has lived in England, Paris and Vancouver before settling down in LA. He studied business and law as well as acting, but luckily for us he chose to pursue the acting side as a career. Phew!

He loves sports, especially extreme sports, and enjoys snowboarding, marathons and Ironman triathlons. Charlie's a guy of extremes, and we think he's an extremely good-looking guy. As some of his fans say, Charlie 'Bewleyful'!

HEART STOPPER!
If you were a fan of Charlie's straight after *New Moon* then you could have called him up – his phone number was still on his website!

HOT-O-METER!

FANG-TASTICALLY CUTE!   THIS VAMP SUCKS!

CHARACTER PROFILE
DEMETRI

CREATED BY: Amun
BORN: Around 1000 AD
TALENTS: Sensory location
OCCUPATION: Volturi guard
ROMANCE: Unknown

Demetri is the Volturi guard with the finely chiseled features. He is tough and lean but incredibly mean! He is the quiet type of guard who doesn't ever say that much and tends to speak with his actions. He is charming and a true gentleman (as far as a vicious Volturi vampire can be!) and is extremely loyal. His true power though, is his ability to track people through their minds. We hope you're tracking this Demetri, because we love you!

DANIEL CUDMORE

BORN: 20 January 1981
PLACE OF BIRTH: Squamish, Canada
STAR SIGN: Aquarius
HEIGHT: 6' 6"
EYE COLOUR: Hazel
HAIR COLOUR: Brown

Daniel has some similarities to Felix, his character in the *Twilight* films. But while they're both wide and strong, Daniel is by far the friendlier of the two! As we can tell from his big, broad build, he's into many sports, and once played American Football for Gannon University.

However, he returned home after breaking his leg and began an acting career instead. Daniel appeared in TV adverts before becoming Colossus in *X-Men 2*. He's as talented as he is tall, so we're sure to see much more of him on our screens soon.

Did you know?

Wearing the vampire contact lenses didn't bother Daniel because he wears contacts in real-life.

HOT-O-METER!

FANG-TASTICALLY **CUTE!**

THIS VAMP **SUCKS!**

CHARACTER PROFILE

F E L I X

PAST NAME: Unknown
BORN: Unknown
CREATED BY: Aro
TALENTS: Strength & fighting
OCCUPATION: Volturi guard
ROMANCE: Unknown

Tall, handsome and broad-shouldered, fit Felix is one ultra-strong vampire guard. He's very imposing and the first to pick a fight, but he also likes to be a bit of a comedian – he's quick with the compliments and always attempts to make the ladies of the Volturi coven laugh.

Large and almost likeable, Felix loves to flirt, and most girls would love to receive a wink from this cheeky, charming character.

Twilight

MOVIE
MOMENTS

Twilight was the one that got us all hooked and looking at these scenes, it's easy to see why.

HERO RESCUE IN PORT ANGELES

Bella leaves the bookshop and is confronted by a group of boys. Edward screeches to her rescue and speeds away in disgust at the thoughts in their heads. Wow! What a hero!

Movie Trivia

The idea for the *Twilight* story came to Stephenie Meyer in a dream. The book was originally called Forks.

Movie Trivia

Smallville's Tom Welling was the fans' original favourite to play the part of Edward.

Quote that!

"This is why we don't show ourselves in the sunlight – people would know we're different."

EDWARD

Movie Trivia

When Stephenie Meyer started writing the first book she didn't have names for Edward and Bella, so she simply called them 'he' and 'she'.

Watch that again!

FIRST KISS

Bella kisses Edward for the first time in her bedroom, until Edward throws himself back against the wall for fear of losing control. They then talk late into the night until Bella falls asleep.

DIAMONDS ARE FOREVER

Edward reveals his true self on the hilltop. A ray of sunlight brushes across him, causing his skin to sparkle like diamonds. Edward declares, 'This is what I am'. If that's what you are, then we love it!

New Moon
MOVIE
MOMENTS

With *New Moon* came some sizzling new scenes. Check out these movie moments.

Quote that!

"I used to be a good kid – not anymore."
JACOB

Movie Trivia

The house used as Jacob's home was originally painted green. The crew had to paint it red to fit the books.

Watch that again!

WOLF'S OUT OF THE BAG!

After Bella confronts the pack, Paul loses his cool and phases right before her eyes. Jacob then leaps from his house and jumps over Bella, phasing as he does, to protect her.

Movie Trivia

Director Chris Weitz provided a pamphlet he'd written to each of the cast to help them grasp his vision.

Movie Trivia

A bay window was added to Bella's bedroom to assist in Jacob jumping in. The bay window didn't exist in *Twilight*.

CRUSHING GOODBYE

It's Bella's birthday and she requests just one thing from Edward . . . a kiss! However, the mood quickly changes. In the scene that follows, Edward explains that he and his family have to leave Forks, a decision that crushes both Bella and himself.

JACOB REVEALS ALL!

Bella takes her new bike for a test drive and tumbles into a rock. With nothing to hand to dab the cut, Jake pulls off his T-shirt and reveals his amazing body for the first time. The next time we see Jake shirtless, he has phased.

Eclipse
MOVIE
MOMENTS

From romance to danger, take a look at these hot scenes from *Eclipse*.

Quote that!

"You wouldn't have to change for me, Bella."
JACOB

Movie Trivia

Location shooting for *Eclipse* took place in British Columbia and Vancouver in Canada.

Movie Trivia

Eclipse director David Slade also directed the vampire movie *30 Days of Night*.

Movie Trivia

All the *Twilight* movies so far have been released in the winter, except *Eclipse*.

Watch that again!

MOUNTAIN KISS

After discovering that Bella has agreed to marry Edward, Jacob threatens to get himself killed in the newborn battle. Nothing Bella can say will convince Jake to stay until she asks him to kiss her. Jake seizes the moment.

JACOB DECLARES HIS LOVE

Jacob declares his love and thrusts himself towards Bella for a kiss. She is shocked and upset and slaps Jake across the face. Back outside Bella's house, Edward squares up to Jacob before Charlie quickly defuses the situation.

THE PROPOSAL

The Cullens leave Forks for the night, leaving Bella to have a sleep-over with Edward. They begin to kiss until Edward stops it. He then gets down on one knee and proposes to Bella whilst handing her his mother's ring.

Breaking Dawn
MOVIE MOMENTS

Breaking Dawn is the finale of the *Twilight* Saga and just when you thought it was all coming to an end, don't fear, the final book will come to the screen in two parts. So, let's take a look at what to expect from the two-part finale.

Breaking Dawn looks set to play host to a whole new breed of hot actors. Not only is there likely to be many additions to the beautiful vampire covens, but a host of hunky new werewolves are set to join the pack and fill the movie screen with muscles. If you loved *Twilight*, *New Moon* and *Eclipse* and you're a fan of Robert, Taylor or any of the boys featured in this book, then you'll be in for a treat. Expect passion, a wedding and a screenful of blood-pumping action.

Quote that!

"It's been my whole life. My whole 20s. And I wouldn't have it any other way."

ROBERT

Movie Trivia

The cast of *Breaking Dawn* are looking forward to partying at the wedding! We are too!

Movie Trivia

Kiowa Gordon, who plays Embry, says he's looking forward to more fierce mayhem between the vampires and werewolves.

A-Z OF Twilight

Take a trip through the immortal alphabet of the Twilight world
and discover the ultimate A-Z of the saga so far.

A	Aro	The leader of the Volturi.
B	Bella	The lamb who falls in love with the lion.
C	Cullen	Carlisle's surname, also given to his adopted children.
D	Demetri	The rather large and strong Volturi guard.
E	Edward	The world's most beautiful vampire.
F	Forks	The real-life town with a population of just over 3000.
G	Glitter	What happens to vampires' skin in direct sunlight.
H	Hale	Rosalie and Jasper's surname.
I	Imprinting	What werewolves do when it's love at first sight.
J	Jasper	The mood-swinging vampire in love with Alice.
K	Kellan	The hunky actor who plays Emmett.
L	La Push	The place where the Quileute live.

Bella

Cullen

Jasper

LA PUSH

FORKS

Volturi

Werewolf

Xavier

M	**Meyer**	Stephenie, the saga's creator.
	Newborns	Newly-transformed vampires.
N O P Q R	**Olympic**	The official name of the Cullen coven.
	Paul	The angry werewolf of the pack.
	Quileute	The name of Jacob's tribe.
	Riley	The leader of Victoria's army.
S T U V W X Y Z	**Seth**	Young member of Quileute tribe.
	Twilight	The story that started the saga.
	Uley	Sam's surname – Alpha of the pack.
	Volturi	The 3000 year old vampire coven.
	Werewolf	The shape-shifting form of the pack.
	Xavier	Xavier Samuel plays Riley.
	Yellow eyes	Veggie vampires have yellow eyes.
	Zafrina	Look out for this vampire in *Breaking Dawn*.

Answers

Page 25 - Vampire Hunt

Page 48 - Spot the Difference

Page 49 - Crossword